"Mardi Gras Evening"

American Accounting Association
Annual Meeting
New Orleans, Louisiana
August, 1998

ᴇᴜ ERNST & YOUNG LLP

NEW ORLEANS

A PICTORIAL SOUVENIR

CAROL M. HIGHSMITH AND TED LANDPHAIR

NEW ORLEANS

A PICTORIAL SOUVENIR

CRESCENT BOOKS

NEW YORK

THE AUTHORS GRATEFULLY ACKNOWLEDGE
THE SERVICES, ACCOMMODATIONS, AND SUPPORT PROVIDED BY
HILTON HOTELS CORPORATION
AND THE NEW ORLEANS RIVERSIDE HILTON AND TOWERS
IN CONNECTION WITH THE COMPLETION OF THIS BOOK.

———

PAGES 2–3:
A modern skyline
would have been
impossible had
engineers not fig-
ured a way to sink
pilings deep into
the city's soupy soil.

This 1998 edition is published by Crescent Books,
a division of Random House Value Publishing, Inc.,
201 East 50th Street, New York, NY 10022.

Crescent Books and colophon are registered trademarks of
Random House Value Publishing, Inc.

Random House
New York • Toronto • London • Sydney • Auckland
http://www.randomhouse.com/

Printed and bound in China

Library of Congress Cataloging-in-Publication Data
Highsmith, Carol M., 1946–
New Orleans / Carol M. Highsmith and Ted Landphair.
p.   cm. — (Pictorial souvenir)
ISBN 0-517-18761-2
1. New Orleans (La.)—Pictorial works.
I. Landphair, Ted, 1942– . II. Title.
III. Series: Highsmith, Carol M., 1946–   Pictorial souvenir.
F379.N543H54   1998
976.3´35—dc21   97–23484
                                                        CIP

8   7   6   5   4   3   2   1

———

Project Editor: Donna Lee Lurker
Production Supervisor: Richard Willett
Designed by Robert L. Wiser, Archetype Press, Inc., Washington, D.C.

FOREWORD

The historic sights, rhythmic sounds, tantalizing tastes, and exotic smells of New Orleans linger with visitors long after they have left the Queen City of the South. The city holds more parades and festivals than there are days in the year. Its citizens parade at funerals and weddings, march in honor of saints and Saints' football victories, and throw exuberant parties to celebrate jazz, blues, French Quarter ambience, and on the slightest of other pretexts. Music is everywhere in New Orleans. It filters out of jazz joints and blues clubs, out of churches, and echoes down the streets as a brass band prances past or a street-corner musician wails on his saxophone.

The Crescent City—thus named because the Mississippi River coils so acutely past town that the sun actually rises over the West Bank in spots—has the saucy ambience of a Caribbean outpost blessed with American amenities. New Orleans is Latin *mañana*, Italian zest, French *joie de vivre*, African-American effervescence, Uptown Creole pomp, all stirred with a dash of southern indolence and a sprinkle of tropical raindrops into a savory cultural gumbo unmatched in the nation. *Laissez les bon temps rouler*—Let the Good Times Roll—is a way of life.

New Orleans delights in its idiosyncrasies. Tombs are aboveground "cities of the dead," owing to soil that is little more than compacted sand. Inhabitants ignore the surgeon general in droves. They smoke, drink alcohol and strong coffee, and jauntily eat things that are bad for them. For the cooking in this city, with its mélange of French, Spanish, Italian, African, and Anglo-Saxon influences, is so delicious, that it draws an international following. At such famous restaurants as Arnaud's, Antoine's, or the original Ruth's Chris steakhouse, a meal is truly a sinful event.

Almost nowhere in this town will you hear the sultry southern accents that actors affect in movies supposedly set in New Orleans. The real accent is more Brooklyn than bayou. And tourists are often surprised not to hear French spoken everywhere. Italian-Americans are the largest white ethnic group in Metropolitan New Orleans. Italians first came here after the American Civil War and, by 1937, almost 80 percent of the "French" Quarter was Italian-owned.

Creole and black cultures are also in full flower in New Orleans. Many Negro slaves bought their freedom in the broad-minded river city as early as 1770, and the community of "free people of color" was the largest in America before the Civil War. Many African Americans here found success through music, especially jazz. The first band known to have played jazz was Buddy Bolden's African-American ensemble in New Orleans in 1895.

New Orleans's major multimillion-dollar draw is its yearly Carnival, a fantasy world unmatched in North America. In a festive ritual, weeks of parades and costume balls culminate on Mardi Gras, or "Fat Tuesday," where masked members of secret societies and social clubs ride on elaborate floats dispensing beads and other trinkets to throngs of revelers.

New Orleans hypnotizes as no other American city can. Painters and photographers are as thick as Louisiana mudbugs (crawfish), and writers flock in to soak up the hedonism. As James Agee wrote: "New Orleans is stirring, rattling, sliding faintly in the fragrance of the enormous riches of its lust." There's no doubt about it; once New Orleans gets in your blood, it's there to stay.

Tile signs identifying Spanish names for streets and landmarks such as Jackson Square (above) can be found throughout the French Quarter. Even though Louisiana Territory was Spanish for only forty-one years, much of the architecture of the Quarter is Spanish, because earlier French buildings were destroyed by fire. The 1799 Cabildo (right) in Jackson Square was the courthouse and center of the last years of Spanish colonial administration. The Cabildo was later home to the Louisiana State Supreme Court, where Plessy v. Ferguson and other landmark cases were argued. Now part of the Louisiana State Museum, the Cabildo houses artifacts from colonial and early Louisiana state history.

New Orleans's best-known landmark, the 1794 Saint Louis Cathedral (left) is America's oldest cathedral. It was a gift to the city from Spanish nobleman Don Andres Almonester y Roxas, who built it "on condition that mass would be said every Sunday in perpetuity after his death for the repose of his soul." Indeed, although tourists often just briefly peek inside the cathedral (opposite), full masses are still held there every day. Clark Mills's equestrian statue of Andrew Jackson, hero of the Battle of New Orleans, is a copy of those in Washington, D.C., and Nashville, Tennessee. Benjamin Butler, the detested commander of occupying Federal forces, ordered the inscription, "The Union must and shall be preserved" carved into its pedestal during the Civil War.

A buggy tour (right) is a leisurely way to enjoy the sights of the French Quarter. Tour guides are exuberant storytellers, though the accuracy of their tales varies greatly. Buggies line up in front of Jackson Square, and others, like this Mid-City Carriage, give customized tours through the Quarter and elsewhere in the city.

Concern over the treatment of mules (above), especially in New Orleans's steamy summers, led to the placement of drinking troughs and strict inspection of the animals' care. The clip-clop of mules' hooves, mingled with distant music and laughter, endures as a "sound souvenir" of pleasurable visits to the romantic old city.

Voodoo tours, readings, drum and chant rituals, and artifacts of the great Voodoo queen, Marie Laveau, are staples at the New Orleans Historic Voodoo Museum in the French Quarter. Visitors can get their own good-luck gris-gris bags of herbs and oils and arrange for spooky tours of swamp country. They can even stay overnight in the "Voodoo Arms" apartments overlooking the museum courtyard. The Vieux Carré is also the place to find fortune tellers like "Madame Michael," who reads palms and tarot cards in front of the Presbytere on Jackson Square. The streets beneath the square's Pontalba Apartments—built by a baroness in 1849—are also lined with artists who sketch visitors in chalk, charcoal, or pencil. Others offer watercolors, oils, and prints of French Quarter scenes.

Until a world-class aquarium opened in the Riverwalk, the shopping pavilion along the Mississippi River on the site of the 1984 Louisiana World's Fair, New Orleans offered few attractions for children. In a way, though, the entire city is an amusement park. Street clowns, like balloon maker Darryl Poché (above), are everywhere. And kids as well as adults can get a fascinating behind-the-scenes look at year-round preparations for the monthlong Carnival celebration by visiting Blaine Kern's Mardi Gras World, across the river from the French Quarter on the West Bank. Here, artisans like Brian Bush (opposite) touch up and restore the hundreds of giant papier-mâché and fiberglass figures—such as Godzilla, Peter Pan, the Creature from the Black Lagoon, and the heads of famous figures like George Washington, Marilyn Monroe, and Frankenstein's monster—that roll in Carnival parades.

French Quarter mimes, like Erod Newton (opposite), are a study in body control. Like the royal guards at London's Buckingham Palace, these human statues delight in outlasting good-natured tormentors. Less flashy mimes have even been mistaken for sculptures. Few street characters' costumes compare, however, to the extravagant ensembles that appear at Carnival. Allen Little (above) is the captain of the "Mystic Krewe of Perseus," one of several Carnival organizations that parades through the streets of New Orleans, surrounding suburbs, and elsewhere in South Louisiana. A krewe captain gets much of the work organizing each year's parade and other events—and little of the glory that a king or queen receives. Still, Little gets to pull out one of his dozen or so elaborate vestments for a day of mirth with fellow Perseus members once a year.

Mardi Gras is often
confused with
Carnival. The latter
is a monthlong
festival of parades
and balls leading
up to Mardi Gras—
"Fat Tuesday"—
the last day of indul-
gence before solemn
Ash Wednesday. On
Mardi Gras, select
Carnival krewes and
hundreds of thou-
sands of merrymakers
dress up, whoop it up,
and soak up the spec-
tacle. "Dr. Rose"—
Tom Perkins—
(right), is a year-
round French Quarter
fixture, but these
unidentified charac-
ters (opposite) are
fixed up just for
Mardi Gras. On
that one day, nearly
everybody but police,
medics, convenience-
store workers, and
clean-up krewes has
the day off for fun.
Hijinks border on
debauchery in the
French Quarter, but
elsewhere it's a day
when families picnic
and youngsters beg
for trinkets from
passing parades.

Bourbon Street on Mardi Gras (left) is a sea of revelry on the street and in balconies above. A walk from Canal Street to the first break in the crowd can take an hour. On any Friday or Saturday night, it's as much fun watching tourists watch the inebriates, uninhibited dancers, and moon-howlers as watching these characters themselves. One of the oldest and most popular Carnival parading organizations is the Krewe of Zulu, whose members (above) roll on Mardi Gras morning. Zulu's "throws" include prized painted Zulu coconuts. Not just on Mardi Gras but also year round in Bourbon Street clubs like the Maison Bourbon (overleaf), Dixieland jazz is the traditional sound of the city. This happy music is characterized by extemporaneous riffs by each band member.

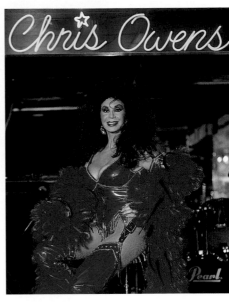

Except in the wee hours, an occasional Sunday morning, or a rare moment before dinnertime when the city seems to take a breath before another wild evening, Bourbon Street (left) is rarely deserted. Tawdry in spots, with ample striptease clubs and adult shops, the feel-good center of "The City that Care Forgot" has a surprising number of good hotels, oyster bars, jazz clubs, and restaurants. In its lower reaches, there are even several blocks of quiet row houses. For a generation, the street's most famous performer and goodwill ambassador has been saucy chanteuse Chris Owens (above), who delights crowds at her club with a rousing—and entirely tasteful—show.

"I've always wanted to play on Bourbon Street," jokes legendary New Orleans pianist Ronnie Kole (opposite). Kole did play Bourbon Street, not literally on the pavement as he does here, but in his own club for years, and once a month since then in the Mystic Den of the Royal Sonesta Hotel. Kole, a classically trained showman slides seamlessly from rollicking boogie-woogie to somber, contemplative numbers. Street musicians like Hack Bartholomew (top right) play an integral part in the sound of the Crescent City as well. So do small ensembles like performers at the popular jazz brunch (bottom right) at Royal Street's Court of Two Sisters. OVERLEAF: Lafitte's Blacksmith Shop is a quaint bar in a photogenic eighteenth-century cottage. According to legend, pirate Jean Lafitte operated a blacksmith shop here as a front for his traffic in contraband seized from captured or wrecked ships.

New Orleans has long been influenced by cultures of the Caribbean, where many wealthy French sugar planters had ties and from which thousands of slaves were brought to the city. One example is the profusion of vivid color on the façades of cottages such as the pink house on lower Bourbon Street (right). In a sense the city is rediscovering this flamboyance, for many homes had faded or deteriorated before being brightly restored. New owners carefully researched the historically correct colors of the c. 1810 "Circle Cottage" on Bourbon Street (above), for instance, before rejuvenating it. They were surprised to discover the original bright red and green hues.

New Orleans residents often enrich their homes with decorative touches, like iron grillework and festive ferns on this Royal Street balcony (above). A Bourbon Street cottage (left) employs the city's symbol— the fleur de lis. Royal Street's Cornstalk Hotel (overleaf) is one of two New Orleans structures— the other is Uptown— enclosed by a cast- iron cornstalk fence entwined with iron morning-glories. The hotel was the home of Francis- Xavier Martin, first chief justice of the Louisiana Supreme Court. The story attributed inter- changeably to the two properties is that the owner's wife missed the rural scenery of the Midwest, so her con- siderate spouse ordered the cornstalk design.

French Quarter balcony apartments like those on Dumaine Street (left and above) are highly prized. They sit serenely above the commotion, are fun to decorate, and give residents a pleasant perch on which to enjoy coffee or a meal. They are also an ideal perch from which to enjoy Carnival or an impromptu parade. First-time guests on these balconies may be stunned to see ships on the Mississippi River passing at eye level, for the streets of the Quarter lie well below the river. New Orleans's gleaming Central Business District (overleaf), viewed from atop the New Orleans Riverside Hilton and Towers, stands in remarkable contrast to the neighboring old Vieux Carré.

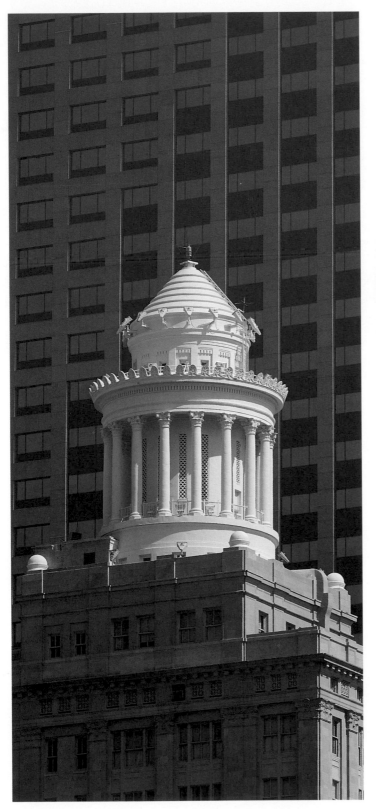

Canal Street (opposite) had fallen on hard times before a vibrant renewal replaced many vacant units and cluttered retail spaces with fine hotels and lively restaurants. The bright-white Hibernia Bank tower (left), which for decades was the most recognizable building on the low-lying New Orleans skyline, is dwarfed by soaring office towers today. In Lafayette Square—the American section's early counterpart to the French Quarter's square—stands a monument to John McDonogh (above), presented to the city by the schoolchildren of New Orleans. McDonogh, a wealthy New Orleans business-man, left his entire fortune to support free schools there and in his native Baltimore.

The sweet sounds of clarinetist Pete Fountain (above) have entertained millions of Dixieland jazz fans on his albums, each Mardi Gras as he leads his "Half-Fast Marching Band" through New Orleans streets, and evenings at his club in the New Orleans Riverside Hilton and Towers. Zesty food and great music come together at the Palace Café on Canal Street. In 1991, as they were converting venerable Oerlein's music store into a lively restaurant and sidewalk café, the owners commissioned artist Marilyn Carter Rougelot to ring the balcony level with a mural featuring New Orleans scenes. In this section (left), piano player "Sweet Emma" and trumpeter Papa Celestin are among the musicians depicted.

New Orleans's Warehouse District, along the Mississippi River but away from French Quarter crowds, had deteriorated into a Skid Row of abandoned factories and storehouses. But the Louisiana World Exposition of 1984 centered there—an artistic success but critical and financial disappointment—led to a stunning neighborhood revitalization. The Riverwalk (above), a half-mile-long shopping arcade, connects with the huge convention center on the old fair site. The delightful Restaurant L'Economie (right) was once The Economy, a blue-collar workers' luncheonette. Artists like Luis Colmenares (opposite) have turned many of the district's warehouses into studios and loft apartments. Colmenares is a "metal artist" who turns scraps of iron, tin, and even silver and gold into highly prized furniture and decorative signs.

Not all of Uptown New Orleans is an enclave of fashionable mansions. The area has a host of old-timey shops and restaurants, including colorful Casamento's seafood restaurant (above) on Magazine Street. There, waitress Alma Griffin serves television personality and newspaper essayist Ronnie Virgets the house specialty—ice-cold "ersters" on the half shell. Once a racing writer with the nom de plume "Railbird Ronnie," Virgets seeks out the "real New Orleans" for his whimsical "Remoulade" television features. He has often stopped at Fred Hahn and Joan Wright's Uptown Fruit Stand (right), which they set up on South Carrollton Avenue in the city's first "streetcar suburb." Save, perhaps for "Jersey" tomatoes from the state of that name, Creole tomatoes are acclaimed as the sweetest in the land.

Uptown's premier restaurant is Commander's Palace, founded in 1880 by Emile Commander and soon patronized by distinguished neighborhood families. But by the 1920s the site was a notorious brothel. It was rehabilitated and, beginning in the 1970s, turned by Ella, Dottie, Dick, and John Brennan into a culinary legend. Commander's features a jazz brunch in its romantic courtyard (opposite) on Saturdays and Sundays. The restaurant, on Washington Avenue, cannot be easily missed: its main building is painted a shocking turquoise— faithful to its color in bawdier days. A few blocks away on Napoleon Avenue, vampire mystery novelist Anne Rice bought Saint Elizabeth's asylum (left), once an orphanage. Even statelier mansions can be found on Saint Charles Avenue (overleaf), down the street.

Tulane and Loyola universities' Uptown campuses (right) are separated by only a hedge. In the foreground is Tulane's Dinwiddie Hall. Behind it is Loyola's Holy Name of Jesus Church, inspired by England's Canterbury Cathedral. The campus church's lofty spires are among the city's most impressive. Loyola, the South's largest Roman Catholic university, moved from a downtown location in 1911. So did private, nonsectarian Tulane seventeen years earlier. It began as the Medical College of Louisiana and was rechristened to honor benefactor Paul Tulane. Tulane's medical school is also in the Central Business District. The Christ and the Samaritan Fountain at Notre Dame Seminary (opposite), around the riverbend on South Carrollton Avenue, was the centerpiece sculpture at the 1984 Louisiana World Exposition's Vatican Pavilion.

Many cottages at the Riverbend in old Carrollton—once a resort favored for its fresh air and river views—are small but distinctive. Some are delicately ornamented (top right). Others are classic "shotgun houses" (bottom right). These are narrow homes, often built as inexpensive rental property, in which rooms follow one behind the other. The name is pure imagery: the idea is that a shotgun blast through the front door would carry straight out the back door. The Pitot House (opposite), named for owner James Pitot, the first elected mayor of New Orleans, is one of the few remaining West Indies-style houses that lined Bayou Saint John in the 1700s. It is not far from resplendent City Park, whose lagoon (overleaf) lures artists, picnickers, and daydreamers.

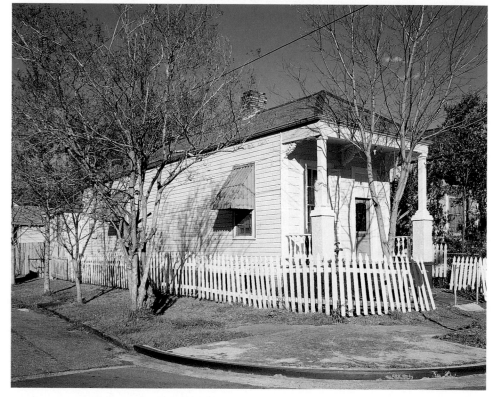

Suburban Metairie contains lavish homes but also some of the area's most congested shopping areas. Many people visit not the living but the dead at the sprawling Metairie Cemetery (right) where, as S. Frederick Starr pointed out in his revealing book of essays called New Orleans UnMasqued, *Confederate heroes and Louisiana luminaries are "at rest above the water table." Metairie's lavish Longue Vue House and Gardens (opposite) is an eight-acre estate once owned by cotton broker Edgar Bloom Stern, who ran Louisiana's first television station, and his wife, Edith, who was the daughter of Sears magnate Julius Rosenwald. Now open for tours and research into architectural and landscape design, Longue Vue features both wild and incomparably cultivated gardens, as well as ponds and outdoor sculptures.*

New Orleans's "back of town" contains some of the city's most idiosyncratic delights, like a mom-and-pop store (top right) that serves the New Orleans equivalent of a submarine or hoagie sandwich: the "po-boy." Usually this epicurean's nightmare is stuffed with Italian lunch meats, roast beef, fried oysters, or shrimp, slathered with mayonnaise, and topped with dashes of pepper sauce. Many musical celebrities have come out of the poor Ninth Ward, where pop singer Antoine "Fats" Domino maintains a home and studio (bottom right). In another poor neighborhood, Trémé, near Congo Square— where slaves were once encouraged to chant and dance for the amusement of their masters—stands a statue that honors another New Orleans superstar, trumpeter Louis Armstrong (opposite). "Satchmo" broke out of poverty to gain worldwide fame.

LOUIS ARMSTRONG

Faubourg Marigny, just downriver from the French Quarter, was a retreat for ruling Creoles and a place where free persons of color owned as much as 40 percent of the cottages. It was developed by a slaveholder, Bernard de Marigny, an enthusiastic duelist who taught the deadly practice to neighboring Americans. The Marigny is now home to a community theater and small businesses, including the big Battistella's Seafood wholesaler (left). America's famous "Cajun Chef," Paul Prudhomme (above), whose restaurant and videotapes introduced his family recipes to an enthusiastic worldwide audience, maintains a homespun test kitchen there.

Titles available in the Pictorial Souvenir series